HOW TO BE A SUCCESSFUL LANDLORD AND PROPERTY INVESTOR

by
Clive Warrington

This book is protected under the copywrite laws. Any reproductions or other unauthorised use of the material herein prohibited without the express written permission of the author.

Copyright © 2020 by Clive Warrington
All rights reserved

ISBN: 9798632246705

Disclaimer

Although the author and publisher have made every effort to ensure that the information in this book was correct at the time of publication, the author and publisher do not assume and hereby disclaim any liability to any party for any loss, damage or disruption from use or misuse of the information provided in this book.

This book relates to renting homes in England and Wales to an individual, couple or family. It does not cover Homes of Multiple Occupancy (HMOs).

For properties in Scotland, in order to rent out, you will need to register with www.landlordregistrationscotland.gov.uk

In order to rent out a property in Wales, you will need to register with Rent Smart Wales, www.rentsmart.gov.wales

Contents

Disclaimer 2

Introduction 4

1. Researching the area 5
2. Deposit 5
3. Renting with and without permissions 5
4. Buy-to-let mortgages 6

    Mortgage interest tax relief changes 8

5. What the mortgage lenders need to hear 8
6. Buying a property 9

    Leasehold Reforms 10

    Building Condition 11

    Putting in an Offer 12

7. Limited Company or Personal Tax 13
8. Get an Accountant 14

    Keep all receipts 14

9. Legal Obligations 15
10. Selective Licensing .... ,,16
11. Trades People 17
12. 'No fault' evictions 17
13. Need or want to Sell 18
14. Letting Agents and Managing Your Property 18
15. If things go wrong with the Letting Agent & the Redress Scheme 21
16. Fees to consider 22
17. Rogue Landlord database 22

    Stamp Duty 23

18. HM Land Registry – protecting your property from fraudsters 23

Final Thoughts 25

Introduction

I have been a successful landlord for over 20 years and have also worked as a mortgage advisor. I therefore have insider information of how mortgage lenders operate and know the requirements to satisfy lending. This book will set you on your journey to becoming a successful landlord. It is an up to date and easy to follow guide and includes the new legislation for 2020 and 2021 as well as other plans being considered. It also contains essential knowledge on how to avoid fraudsters selling or taking loans on any property you own.

If you are looking for a way to secure your future then property investment could be the answer. There is a massive shortage of housing; which over time will only worsen. Becoming a successful landlord is surprisingly straight forward and this book will provide you with all the basic details you will need to set up and have a successful portfolio. Even during uncertain times; property continues to be a sound investment.

I became what is known as an 'accidental landlord'. When I was getting married; I found that I had an additional property and wondered whether to rent it. I was a little apprehensive at first but decided to go for it. Since then, I have gone on to buy multiple properties. The lovely cottage on the book cover is part of my rental portfolio.

This book is an uncomplicated, basic guide to the things you need to know to become a successful landlord. I have used the mistakes I have made along the way to write an honest account of how you can give up work and/or have a steady extra income stream. It is not based upon profit alone; I strongly believe that it is important to provide safe and decent housing to tenants. I will take you through the process, from the initial idea to buying and renting your property.

1. Researching the area

You will need to research the area where you plan to buy. Firstly, you will need to decide who you plan to rent to; professionals, for example. This will determine the areas that you look to buy property. Young professionals will tend to want to be close to vibrant town or city areas, whereas families usually prefer quieter suburban areas.

Keep an eye on property prices in areas you find interesting and speak to a few Letting Agents to obtain their views; they know the market and the anticipated achievable rent. Consider factors like the proximity to transport links, local amenities and schools etc.

2. Deposit

Unless buying outright, you will need a deposit and a mortgage. The standard required deposit is typically 25%; a higher deposit, however, will grant you access to more favourable mortgage deals.

3. Renting with and without permissions

As already stated, I became an accidental landlord. If you are in the same position and plan to rent out your home; you will need to obtain permission from your mortgage lender (and the freeholder, if the property is leasehold) and convert your mortgage to a buy-to-let mortgage. You will need to obtain landlords insurance (buildings cover only) as the contents insurance will be provided by the tenant(s) and you will also need to declare your earnings as income. The temptation is, of course, to rent out your property and take the income with nobody else involved or needing to know. However tempting this may appear, **do not ever take this option**!

Now let's think critically about what could happen should you rent without the correct permissions:
. The property burns down – did you know that you will not only be liable for any outstanding mortgage balance but may also have to pay for the rebuild costs?
. There is no way your insurance will pay out as you have residential insurance as far as they are concerned
. HMRC may investigate you for non-payment of tax and there will be heavy penalties
. The tenant stops paying rent to you, this could be a huge problem for you if you take your tenant to court and it is found that you have not done something strictly by the book.

I think it is fair to say that these risks are not worth taking.

4. Buy-to-let mortgages

Buy-to-let mortgage products are less favourable than for residential mortgages and a lot of lenders will require you to have an income of approximately £20,000 (or more). If you do not have this income level right now, you need to think about how you can boost it to the required level. You could consider getting a second job (or primary job, if your income is from other means) which may only be a short-term measure in order to satisfy the mortgage lender that you have a regular income. You could then quit your job once you have the portfolio of properties you want. However, unlike residential mortgages, the most important factor is the income the property generates rather than what you earn so some mortgage lenders will factor this in as income.

Once you have 4 or more properties, you are considered to be a 'Portfolio Landlord' and slightly more rigorous checks are done.

As a guide, lenders will want the rent to be at least 125% (145% if you are a portfolio landlord) of what the mortgage payment would be if the interest rate would be 5.5%.

A buy-to let mortgage is viewed as a business and although your expenditure is assessed (bills, council tax, food, insurance, petrol etc.), the yield that you will receive is also very important. To work out the yield it is very simple to calculate and an expected yield should be anything over 5%.

First, find your annual rental income for the property, then; divide this by the property value. Finally, multiply the figure by 100 to obtain the yield.

$$\text{Yield} = \frac{\text{Annual Rental Income}}{\text{Property Value}} \times 100$$

For example:

. the value of the property is £140,000

. So, if your annual rental income is £7800 and the property is valued at £140,000, your rental yield would be approximately 5.6%.

The mortgage you choose should be an 'Interest Only' mortgage. This will mean that you pay the interest on the loan only and will therefore owe the full amount that you borrow at the end of the mortgage term.

The reason for an 'Interest Only' mortgage as opposed to 'Capital and Repayment' is that your aim is to make a profit and this is the only feasible way to do so. You will need to decide on whether you find a mortgage yourself of go via a broker. Some brokers will charge directly and some are 'free' and live off commissions for the products they sell. There are currently lots of great deals with UK interest rates being low and a fixed rate may be an option if you are a little nervous. Types of mortgages are:

. Fixed Rates – Fixed for a set period of 2, 3, 5 or 10 years. In 2020, there are currently some great 5 year and even 10 year buy-to-let mortgage deals.

. Discounted Mortgages – you pay the lender's standard variable rate (a rate chosen by the lender that doesn't change very often), with a fixed amount discounted. For example, if your lender's standard variable rate is 4% and your mortgage came with a 1.5% discount, you'd pay 2.5%.

. Tracker - With a tracker mortgage, your interest rate 'tracks' the Bank of England base rate.

. Standard Variable Rate - each lender has its own standard variable rate (SVR) that it can set at whatever level it wants. This means that it's not directly linked to the Bank of England base rate. Standard Variable Rates are often the highest rate you will pay so as soon as you can, **switch to a better product.**

Mortgage interest tax relief changes

The Government has been phasing out tax relief on mortgage interest since April 2017, with the proportion you're allowed to deduct slowly being reduced each tax year. From the start of the 2020-21 tax year, you/your accountant will be able to subtract a flat credit of 20% of your mortgage expenses from your rental income when filing your tax return. These changes to tax relief are controversial and many landlords have exited the market because of this alone.

You may at this point be questioning whether to proceed and what I would say is that it is still lucrative and well worth proceeding.

5. What the mortgage lenders need to hear

Before you do anything; check your credit score. There may be something on it in error which may need correcting. There are many companies which offer free credit checks, some have fees after 30 days so be sure to cancel any subscription before the 30 days.

Most residential mortgages have an age limit (typically 65 to 70 years old or your retirement age). This does not concern me because I've worked professionally with mortgages and know the criteria mortgage lenders require. You will be asked when you plan to retire. To answer this question and to ensure that you get a 25-year mortgage, just add 25 years to your age. I am still buying houses in my 50s and I just say that my planned retirement age will be 85 as I know this is all they need to hear.

You will also be asked how you intend on paying back the loan after 25 years, you can say 'sale of the property', again, this is all they need to hear. Quite rightly, you may at this stage be concerned about how you do responsibly pay the loan after 25 years; this can be done by 2 ways:

1. Sell the property after 25 years. The likelihood is that the property would have increased significantly (look back at house prices overall over the past 20 years).

2. Paying small amounts off whenever you can – even mortgages which have a lock-in period usually still allow an overpayment allowance of typically 10% per year without penalties. I would encourage doing this whenever possible.

6. Buying a property

After speaking to letting agents and researching your area; think about the type of property you are looking for. Remember that the rental yield is important for both a good investment and to meet the lending criteria. You can also access (via sites such as Rightmove and Zoopla) the price that a house previously sold for and what other properties on the same road and in the same area have sold for.

You can often see photographs from the previous sale and can therefore compare the improvement works which have been done. Drive around the area at different times of the day/weekend to see the impact of traffic etc. I like to buy properties in the winter; this way I can see whether the heating is working and look for damp etc. An ideal day for viewing is on a rainy day, you can check for leaks etc. Open and close windows and doors, if you have difficulty doing this, the property may have subsided.

Look at the property from a distance; are there any trees in the immediate vicinity of the property which could cause issues? Look at whether the window and door frames are at an angle as this could suggest subsidence. Take binoculars to check out the roof – or use the camera on your smartphone to take a photo and zoom into the picture on a good monitor - to look for damage, missing tiles and the state of the chimney.

You will need to consider whether the tenure of the property is Freehold or Leasehold:

. *Freehold* you own the property and land

. *Leasehold* you own the property but not the land it is built on.

For leasehold properties, you will have charges such as ground rent and possibly service charges for buildings insurance and/or common-area maintenance. You will also need to factor in the years that are remaining on the lease as some lenders will not lend on short leaseholds; particularly 80 years or less. Flats are often sold as leasehold but with flats you can only buy a share of the freehold. You can informally approach the freeholder to negotiate charges. If the freeholder ignores you or you cannot locate the freeholder, there is a process to follow and I would urge you to instruct a solicitor to act on your behalf.

Leasehold Reforms

The Government is attempting to stop unfair leasehold practices from 2020 such as spiralling ground rent clauses and high permission fees. This could also involve the banning of new houses being sold as leasehold as well as caps on service charges, permission fees and ground rents. The Competition and Markets Authority is currently investigating whether existing leasehold homeowners were mis-sold their properties. Leaseholders have a legal right under the Leasehold Reform Act 1967 to buy the freehold of their property if they meet certain qualifying criteria.

The uncertainty in this area means that you should pay particular attention to the tenure of any properties you plan to buy.

Building Condition

Most mortgage lenders will not lend unless the property has a functional bathroom and kitchen. However undesirable you think the existing kitchen and bathroom is, this should not concern you at the buying stage. The absence of a kitchen and bathroom renders the property uninhabitable in the eyes of lenders and you would generally need cash to buy such a property. If you have the money to make a cash purchase, you can recoup it by mortgaging the property when it has been renovated.

Also, properties which are classed as non-standard construction are often only dealt with by specialist mortgage companies. A non-standard construction house is built from materials that do not conform to the 'standard' definition. Standard houses have brick or stone walls with a roof made of slate or tile. A non-standard construction is therefore anything that falls outside of this; examples include houses which are made of concrete or are steel framed.

Once you have viewed a property, you may wish to put in an offer; think about how much the house is worth to you; have a maximum amount you are prepared to offer and do not exceed this amount. Ensure that there is a viable option for a good return – i.e. a yield above 5%.

Putting in an Offer

Before putting in any offer, I would get an 'Offer in Principle' from your preferred lender which will reflect roughly how much you can borrow. You will then be fairly confident that you will get the required amount for borrowing and have the required deposit. The seller (vendor) will also take your offer seriously.

You are also in a strong position if you do not have anything to sell. Vendors are often much happier with investors as there will be no chain. I have, in the past, bought a house much lower than the asking price as I could prove I had a mortgage offer in principle. I was able to show the Estate Agent proof of deposit by showing a recent bank statement and this put me in a strong position to have my low offer accepted.

So, you have your offer accepted. Congratulations!

You will now have to let your proposed lender know that the offer was accepted for an official offer to be made to you. This will typically take 2-3 weeks.

You will need to find a conveyancing solicitor and await further instructions. Be wary about using solicitors recommended by mortgage lenders, quite often they are not solicitors, so unless you want to act as a solicitor with decisions falling to you, find a qualified conveyancing solicitor who will do everything properly.

Your mortgage lender will arrange for a valuation survey to be done; this will be a basic survey to assess the value of the property. After all, nobody will lend you money on a property which is not valued at what you've offered. I usually go for a Home Buyers Report using a RICS qualified surveyor. This will typically cost £500 on a 2 bedroomed house priced at £170,000. Your mortgage lender can arrange this but you can also source this yourself.

The report you receive will be detailed and will show works or repairs needed. Some buyers will use this report to renegotiate their offer based upon the required works needed. If the property is very old or you have concerns, you should opt for a structural survey which will cost more than the Home Buyers Report and is much more detailed.

7. Limited Company or Personal Tax

Buy-to-let mortgages can now be obtained as a limited company and more lenders are now offering these mortgages. Tax is paid as Corporation Tax (which is lower than Personal Tax). Companies pay Corporation Tax at a fixed rate irrespective of the size of the profits.

The Corporation Tax rate has remained at 19%. The Government's plan had been to reduce this tax to 17% in 2020, however, the budget set on 11th March 2020 left the rate at 19%.

This can still be very attractive compared to 40% for higher rate tax payers and 45% for additional higher rate taxpayers.

The question is how the money in the company is passed to the individual. If the money is taken out of the company as a dividend; only the first £2,000 of dividend income is tax free. Any dividends taken out in excess of this will be charged at:

. Basic-rate taxpayers pay 7.5% on dividends
. Higher-rate taxpayers pay 32.5% on dividends
. Additional-rate taxpayers pay 38.1% on dividends

This tax is paid on dividends after the corporation tax at 19% has been paid.

The money could be taken as a salary; however, the company would have to operate PAYE and pay Employers National

Insurance contributions on any salaries paid. This usually works out more expensive than paying dividends.
There are also advantages of not having a limited company and paying Personal Tax. Think about your income/pension and if you have little or no provisions, you can take advantage of your personal tax allowance which is currently over £12,500 per annum. This means you can earn this amount before paying any tax.

There is also a Capital Gains benefit (should you sell the property) if you go via the Personal Tax route which is currently over £12,000 per person for any profit before any tax is payable.

You should obtain sound financial advice from either an accountant or tax advisor before you make your choice of which is best for you.

8. Get an Accountant

Unless you know about accounts, you should get an accountant. You can of course learn how to do your own accounts but I would advise against this. Your accountant will have up to date knowledge of the laws and tax changes and this information is vital in order to pay the correct amount and work within the law.

Having proof of accounts will also help you buy additional properties as lenders will ask for the previous years' accounts when assessing future lending, particularly if you have a few buy-to-let mortgages.

Keep all receipts: your accountant will be able to tell you whether the costs can be offset against tax or whether they can be claimed back when you sell the property. The accountant's invoice can also be offset as an expense.

9. Legal Obligations

There are some current legal obligations to consider:

. Gas Safety Certificate - If the property you let out has gas, you will need an annual Gas Safety Certificate carried out by a qualified Gas Safety Engineer. The Gas safety Register (which replaced Corgi in 2009) has a register for all qualified engineers who can be found on the Gas safety Register website: https://www.gassaferegister.co.uk/

. Energy Performance Certificates - energy efficiency rules from April 2020 require more landlords to meet the new Minimum Energy Efficiency Standard regulations.

There are some exemptions such as holiday accommodation, listed buildings etc. Most rented properties, however, will have to have a minimum Energy Performance Certificate (EPC) rating of 'E'. Landlords with properties that do not meet the regulations must carry out energy efficiency measures on their homes, up to a cap of £3,500 per property.
The rules were first introduced in 2018 but originally only covered new tenancies and renewals. From April 2020, these rules apply to _all_ existing tenancies. Discussions are also taking place to further increase the EPC rating to 'D' in 2025.

You should also look at the EPC rating of any property you intend on buying to ensure you are buying a property with an 'E' rating or above. There will be heavy fines for being non-compliant which runs into £1000s. The certificates last for 10 years so if you already have rental properties, you must remember to renew these when necessary too.

Energy Performance Certificates can be viewed and downloaded free of charge on the EPC Register: https://www.epcregister.com/

. Electrical Safety Check - Mandatory five-year electrical safety check regulations are to be enforced in England. The draft regulations propose that, from 1 July 2020, all new private tenancies in England will need to ensure that electrical installations are inspected and tested by a qualified person before the tenancy begins. For existing tenancies, an electrical safety test will need to be carried out by 1 April 2021.

These costs can be offset against tax. I would also suggest having smoke alarms fitted and also carbon monoxide sensors where appropriate. These are likely to be mandatory at some point so you should put these in place for safety reasons. You could also consider joining an Association for Landlords.

10. Selective Licensing

This is something which a few councils are introducing or piloting in some areas of England. I am currently going through this process for one of my properties. The idea behind this is for there to be a minimum standard for landlords before a property can be rented, to drive out rogue landlords.

I have 6 months to apply for the license and the cost for me will be approximately £800. The license will last for 5 years and during this time; the local council will visit the property to quality check it. These costs can be claimed back and offset against tax and you can usually reduce this cost by being part of a Landlords Association.

The process does not seem as onerous as I first thought and the local council has provided the necessary paperwork online. Should you find yourself affected by this at any time, you are likely to need:

. A copy of the gas safety certificate
. A copy of a valid electrical report
. An information sheet about the mortgage company
. A smoke alarm safety/fire risk assessment
. An energy performance certificate (as referred above under Legal Obligations)

. A fit and proper person confirmation (the local council provides a template)

11. Trades People

Over time, you will build up contacts and will hopefully have good relations with trades people. This is important as they will help you out when needed; sometimes at short notice.

Recommendations from people who have had work carried out is always of benefit. Choose professionals that can provide receipts, as these will be needed as both proof of works and for expenses to be offset against tax.

Always check that trades people have Professional Indemnity Insurance, reputable trades people should be happy to show this to you. I would suggest that you (initially) obtain at least 3 quotes for any work, though you can relax this once you have established a reliable 'team'.

Finally, always pay your invoices promptly. Trades people will be willing to fit your work in, at short notice, if you reliably pay quickly.

12. 'No fault' evictions

Section 21 evictions were a major topic of debate at the end of 2019. The Government consulted on repealing Section 21 of the Housing Act. Section 21 allows landlords to end a 'rolling' tenancy with 2 months' notice, without giving any reason for doing so.

The Government believes repealing Section 21 will offer tenants greater security but landlords fear the proposed changes could mean they have to take troublesome tenants to court to repossess homes.

The National Landlords Association says the proposals are 'ill thought through' and that Section 21 should remain, unless the rules around evicting problematic tenants are reviewed. During the time I have been a landlord, I have only had to serve a Section 21 eviction once and I did this with legal advice.

13. Need or want to Sell

Further to the 'no fault' evictions, a concern you may now have is what to do should you want or need to sell the property quickly. This may be at times of emergency or you simply want to sell.

If a property is tenanted, you will need to serve notice, typically 2 months. There has been some media attention to this, speculating that landlords cannot ask tenants to leave without valid reasons. Of course, tenants need some level of protection but nobody can prevent you from selling your own property at any time.

Therefore, all you need to say is that you plan to sell the property and serve notice citing this as the reason. Whether you then decide to sell or not is simply up to you. Should you decide to sell your property after a few years and/or have updated the property; you are highly likely to have made a good return too.

14. Letting Agents and Managing Your Property

Letting Agents will keep you up to date on legislation and mandatory obligations. Most letting agents provide services for both finding a tenant and managing your property by way of an Assured Shorthold Tenancy.

I would advise you to use a letting agent in some format to ensure that you will have done things in the correct manner;

which will be crucial should you need to take any legal action. The Assured Shorthold Tenancy agreement will be for a minimum contract of 6 months. After this time, you do not need to update the contract as it will roll on until the tenant or you give notice to end the tenancy.

Tenants are responsible for paying bills in accordance with the tenancy agreement, these could include: council tax, utility payments (gas, electricity, water, broadband, telephone etc.).

Inventory - I would suggest that you have an inventory done at this time too. A Letting Agent can arrange this and will use a third party to do this so that there is no bias and you/ the tenant will receive a copy at the beginning and end of each tenancy. This is a protection for you should any damage take place which can then be clearly evidenced and the tenant will need to rectify/ possibly lose part/their deposit on the property in order to rectify.

Tenant's deposit - A Letting Agent can also deal with the tenant's deposit which has to be put into a Deposit Protection Scheme (DPS) which is independent. New rules introduced in April 2019 mean that all letting agents in England must belong to a Client Money Protection Scheme. This provides insurance to landlords and tenants alike against malpractice from agents. Agents in Wales and Scotland also need to belong to a scheme as part of the Rent Smart Wales and Letting Agent Code of Practice respectively.

Right to Rent - The Government's Right to Rent initiative has provoked a lot of debate since being launched in 2016. Right to Rent requires landlords to check whether tenants have the right to live in the UK, with the threat of criminal sanctions for those who fail to adhere. In March 2019; the policy was ruled incompatible with human rights law by the High Court after an immigrant welfare group raised a legal challenge. As part of the ruling, Right to Rent cannot be rolled out in Scotland, Wales or Northern Ireland without further evaluation. A letting agent can deal with this check on your behalf.

Permitted Payments

From 1 June 2019, if you or a letting agent enter into a tenancy agreement, student let, or 'licence to occupy housing' in the private rented sector, you will be prohibited from charging any fees or other payments that are not included in the list of permitted payments.

The only charges you can make in connection with a tenancy are:

a) The rent

b) A refundable tenancy deposit capped at no more than five weeks' rent where the annual rent is less the £50,000 or six weeks' rent where the total annual rent is £50,000 or above

c) A refundable holding deposit (to reserve a property) capped at no more than one week's rent

d) Payments to change the tenancy when requested by the tenant, capped at £50, or reasonable costs incurred if higher

e) Payments associated with early termination of the tenancy, when requested by the tenant

f) Payments in respect of utilities, communication services, TV licence and council tax; and

g) A default fee for late payment of rent and replacement of a lost key/security device, where required under a tenancy agreement

Prohibited Payments

If a fee you are charging is not on this list, it is a prohibited payment and you or a letting agent should not be charging it. A prohibited payment is a payment outlawed under the ban.

With effect from 1 June 2020, the ban on fees will apply to all applicable tenancies and licences to occupy housing in the private rented sector. You will not be able to charge any fees after this date; apart from those fees which are expressly permitted under the ban.

15. If things go wrong with the Letting Agent & the Redress Scheme

There is a redress scheme, which is an impartial complaints resolution service, allowing tenants and landlords to raise complaints against their letting agent where the agent has not satisfactorily resolved that complaint. According to the Consumer Rights Act 2015, every letting agent must belong to a Government-approved redress scheme. There are two redress schemes:

. The Property Redress Scheme
. The Property Ombudsman

Letting agents must display the name of the scheme they belong to in their offices and on their website. You can also check that the letting agent is a member of a scheme online:

. https://www.tpos.co.uk/find-a-member
. https://www.theprs.co.uk/consumer/members/

If your agent does not belong to a Government-approved redress scheme, they could face a financial penalty of up to £5,000.

The Tenant Fees Act extends the requirement to display fees to cover online property websites that advertise properties to let on behalf of letting agents.

You should consider seeking independent advice before making a claim for the repayment of a prohibited payment.

Your local authority, redress scheme or the charity Citizens Advice should not charge for their service.

I use a letting agent to find a tenant only; the agent will find a tenant, do the necessary credit and eligibility checks, deal with the tenant's deposit, arrange the inventory and set up the direct debit. Should you wish for the letting agent to also manage your property; management service charges are typically 10-15 % of the monthly rental.

This could be an option for you if you live a long distance from the property or simply do not want to be directly involved with tenants, maintenance issues or annual obligations. Whether you choose to manage your property yourself or do this via an agent is your choice but any charges are classed as expenses and can therefore be offset for tax purposes.

16. Fees to consider

To buy a property, the fees you need to consider:

. Stamp duty – there is an additional 3% to pay
. Solicitor fees for legal work and searches etc
. Mortgage fees on some products

17. Rogue Landlord Database

The rogue landlord database has not taken off to date. A Freedom of Information request found that only four landlords were added to the database in its first year. In July 2019, the Government announced plans to open up the database to tenants, allowing them to check whether their landlord or managing agent was included.

Following this, the Government launched a consultation into reforming the database, which closed in October 2019 and the results are currently being analysed.

Stamp Duty

Stamp duty has been towards the top of the list of landlord gripes since 2016, when the Government introduced a 3% buy-to-let stamp duty surcharge for property investors. From March 2020; there is also a stamp duty surcharge of 2% for foreign buyers investing in UK property. Stamp duty is an area of political interest for landlords and is something to keep an eye on.

18. HM Land Registry – protecting your property from fraudsters

There have been some cases of properties being sold or loans taken out against a property by fraudsters. These cases, although rare, usually take place when landlords are living abroad.

The Land Registry offers a free service portal to register your property for alerts. This system will alert you should there be any activity linked to your property, be it a solicitor making an enquiry or an application for a loan linked to the property. I think that it is very important for you to register all properties that you own with this service and should you have a query, the Land Registry respond swiftly via telephone also.
You do not need to own a property in order to register it. The website and telephone details are:
https://propertyalert.landregistry.gov.uk or 0300 006 0478.

You will receive quite a few alerts when you first purchase a property. This is due to your mortgage company registering their charge with the property and previous lenders removing their details.

Things you need to consider prior to registering are:

. The property you wish to monitor must be situated in England or Wales and registered with HM Land Registry

. You must create a Property Alert account to use the service
. You will receive a HM Land Registry e-mail (check spam inbox) to enable you to verify your e-mail details

. You must then sign in to your account to add a property
. E-mail alerts are sent when official searches and applications are received against a monitored property

. If you receive an alert about activity that seems suspicious, you should take swift action. The alert e-mail will signpost you to who to contact.

. The same property can be monitored by different people

. Property, especially flats/apartments can be registered with two titles. Blocks of flats are often owned by companies (Freehold) and the person owning the individual flat (Leasehold). When registering for this service, choose Leasehold title for individual flats/apartments.

. You can use the service if you are not online, contact the Property Alert team on 0300 006 0478

Owning A Property

Once you have your property, you will need to contact:

. Local Council to let them know you are responsible for the council tax property from the date you own the property until it is let out and between lets. Some Councils allow empty or properties being refurbished an exemption period but this varies from a few months to nothing at all. Any council tax charges can be claimed as expenses offset against tax

. Utilities, Water, Telephone, Gas, Electricity (take meter readings) and transfer to your name until the tenant moves in. Take meter readings again just before the tenant moves in. If an inventory is being done, this should be shown on the inventory report but it is best to note the readings yourself.

Final Thoughts

To conclude; I will always advocate presenting a lovely, clean and safe property for your tenant(s). I pride myself on providing excellent housing and this also has the added benefit of attracting long tenancies.

Good luck with your venture!

Clive

www.ingramcontent.com/pod-product-compliance
Lightning Source LLC
Chambersburg PA
CBHW050329220526
45465CB00005B/2200